ASTRONOMER

by R.J. Bailey

po go

Ideas for Parents and Teachers

Pogo Books let children practice reading informational text while introducing them to nonfiction features such as headings, labels, sidebars, maps, and diagrams, as well as a table of contents, glossary, and index.

Carefully leveled text with a strong photo match offers early fluent readers the support they need to succeed.

Before Reading

- "Walk" through the book and point out the various nonfiction features. Ask the student what purpose each feature serves.
- Look at the glossary together. Read and discuss the words.

Read the Book

- Have the child read the book independently.
- Invite him or her to list questions that arise from reading.

After Reading

- Discuss the child's questions. Talk about how he or she might find answers to those questions.
- Prompt the child to think more. Ask: Do you know anyone who works as an astronomer? What projects has he or she been involved in? Do you have any interest in this kind of work?

Pogo Books are published by Jump!
5357 Penn Avenue South
Minneapolis, MN 55419
www.jumplibrary.com

Copyright © 2018 Jump!
International copyright reserved in all countries.
No part of this book may be reproduced in any form without written permission from the publisher.

Library of Congress Cataloging-in-Publication Data

Names: Bailey, R.J., author.
Title: Astronomer / by R.J. Bailey.
Description: Minneapolis, MN: Jump!, Inc., [2017]
Series: STEM careers | Audience: Ages 7-10.
Includes bibliographical references and index.
Identifiers: LCCN 2017006392 (print)
LCCN 2017007794 (ebook)
ISBN 9781620317129 (hardcover: alk. paper)
ISBN 9781624965890 (ebook)
Subjects: LCSH: Astronomy—Vocational guidance—Juvenile literature. | Astronomers—Juvenile literature.
Classification: LCC QB51.5 .B35 2017 (print)
LCC QB51.5 (ebook) | DDC 520.23—dc23
LC record available at https://lccn.loc.gov/2017006392

Editor: Jenny Fretland VanVoorst
Book Designer: Michelle Sonnek
Photo Researcher: Michelle Sonnek

Photo Credits: Alamy: Stocktrek Images, Inc., 8-9. Getty: Dave King, 1. iStock: RichardVandenberg, 10; shaunl, 19; Mint Images, 20-21. NASA: CXC/SAO/STScI/JPL-Caltech, 12; Marshall Space Flight Center, 13. Shutterstock: Igor Zubkis, cover; Claudio Divizia, cover; Ronnachai Palas, 3; nednapa, 3; MaszaS, 4; Traveller Martin, 5; Mopic, 6-7; michaeljung, 10; Rocketclips, Inc., 12-13; Minerva Studio, 14-15; arka38, 18; Africa Studio, 18; Rawpixel.com, 23. SuperStock: imageBROKER, 11; Hemis.fr, 16-17.

Printed in the United States of America at Corporate Graphics in North Mankato, Minnesota.

TABLE OF CONTENTS

CHAPTER 1

SPACE STUDENTS

Do you like looking at the stars? Do you wonder what else might be out there? People have studied the sky for thousands of years. But there is still much to learn.

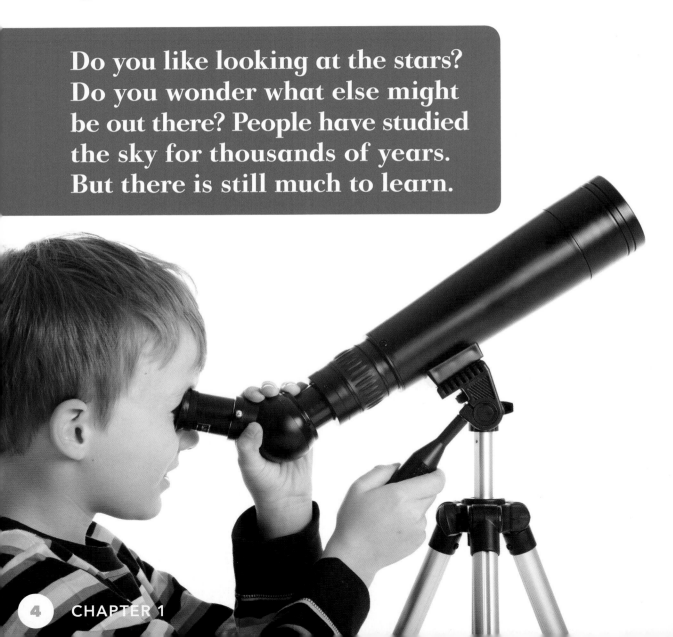

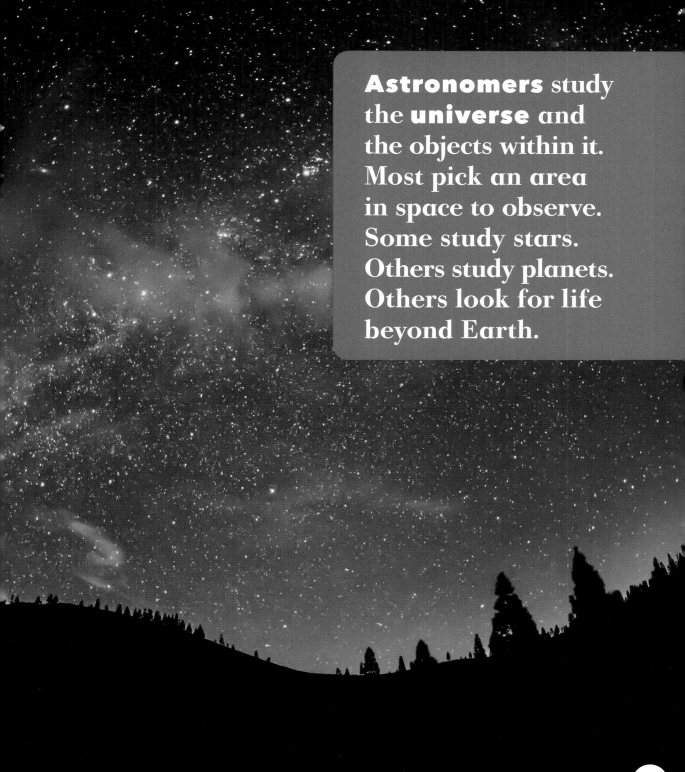

Astronomers study the **universe** and the objects within it. Most pick an area in space to observe. Some study stars. Others study planets. Others look for life beyond Earth.

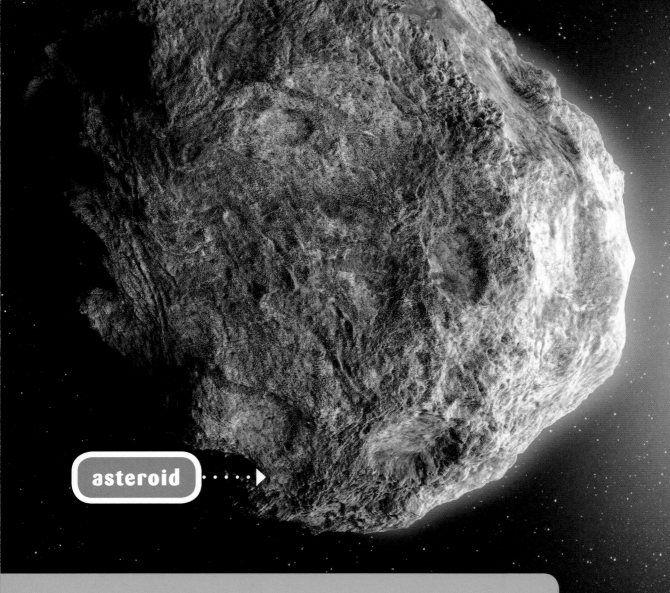

asteroid ·····▶

Astronomers study our **solar system**. They look for **comets**. They look for **asteroids**. Some asteroids are big. They could hit Earth. It is important to know whether we are in one's path!

TAKE A LOOK!

Our solar system is made up of the sun and the planets that move around it.

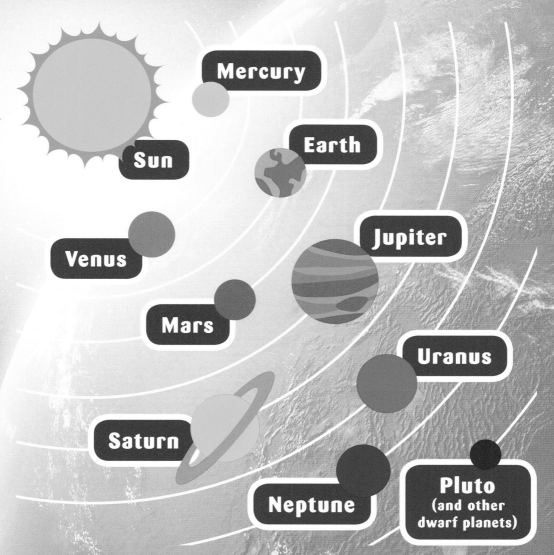

Sun

Mercury

Earth

Venus

Jupiter

Mars

Uranus

Saturn

Neptune

Pluto
(and other
dwarf planets)

galaxy

Astronomers are detectives. They investigate **galaxies**. They discover how they form. They look for **black holes**. Black holes can't be seen. Why? They do not reflect light. But they affect nearby stars and planets. Astronomers look for unusual activity around the stars and planets. This helps them find the black holes.

CHAPTER 2

WHAT DO THEY DO?

It takes a long time for the light from distant stars to reach us. In fact, when you look up at the sky, you are seeing the past! How do astronomers study things that are so far away?

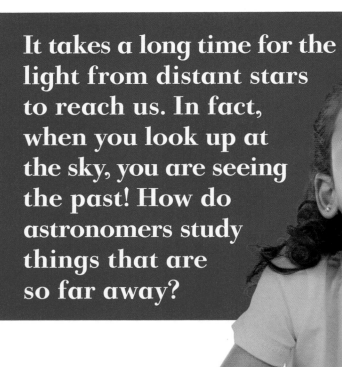

They use powerful **telescopes** to see far into space. Telescopes gather light from distant objects. Many telescopes are on Earth. Some are in buildings called **observatories**.

telescope

Other telescopes are in space. They have cameras on them. They gather **data**.

Astronomers use computers to study the data. They determine the sizes and shapes of objects they see. They determine their brightness. They **simulate** things that could happen in space. Then they advance ideas based on what they learn. They present them at meetings. They write about them in journals.

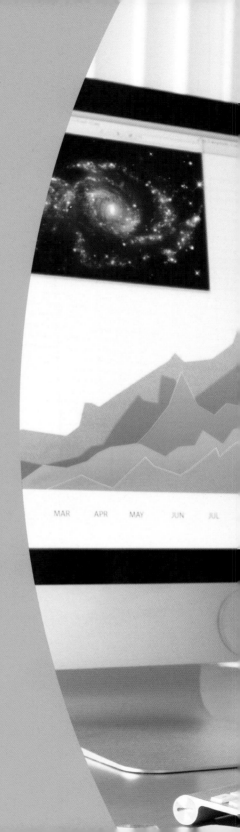

MAR   APR   MAY   JUN   JUL

DID YOU KNOW?

The Hubble is one of the most famous space telescopes. It was sent to space in 1990. Since then it has made more than 1.3 million observations!

Astronomers work with other scientists and **engineers**. They help design equipment for space travel. They plan trips to other planets. They help people understand why these trips are important.

Many astronomers work for government labs. Others teach at universities. Some work in **planetariums**. Others work at science museums. Some work for companies that make telescopes and other instruments for space.

CHAPTER 3

BECOMING AN ASTRONOMER

Do you want to be an astronomer? You need to work hard. In school, take as much math and science as you can. You will need computer and writing skills. You will need good grades. Knowing how to program a computer helps, too!

You also need a college degree. Most astronomers have an advanced degree in astronomy or **physics**. It is called a **Ph.D.**

As an astronomer, you can shape the future. What can you do? Learn as much as you can about the sun. It affects our climate. It can affect our **power grids**. Learn about other planets. Someday you may call Mars home!

DID YOU KNOW?

To work as an astronomer, you need STEM skills. What does STEM stand for? Science. Technology. Engineering. Math. STEM careers are in demand. They pay well, too.

ACTIVITIES & TOOLS

MAKE A TELESCOPE

Do you want to get a better look at the stars or moon at night? If you don't have a telescope, you can make one!

What You Need:
- two paper towel tubes
- scissors
- masking tape
- two convex lenses from two magnifying glasses (one should be slightly larger than the other)

❶ **Cut one paper towel tube lengthwise on one side. Fold one side of the cut edge a little bit over the other.**

❷ **Tape the cut edge down with masking tape.**

❸ **Put this tube inside the second paper towel tube. It should fit tightly, but you should be able to slide this inner tube in and out of the outer tube.**

❹ **Tape the smaller lens to the outer edge of the inner tube. Tape just around the rim of the lens.**

❺ **Tape the larger lens to the outer edge of the larger tube.**

❻ **At night, hold your telescope with the inner tube facing your eye. Aim it at an object in the sky. Focus your telescope by slowly sliding the inner tube in and out. What do you see?**

GLOSSARY

asteroids: Small, rocky objects orbiting the sun.

astronomers: Scientists who study the universe and the objects within it.

black holes: Invisible areas in space with a strong gravitational pull.

comets: Bright objects in space that have a cloudy tail as they move closer to the sun.

data: Facts about something.

engineers: People who use math and science to solve society's problems and create things that humans use.

galaxies: Large groups of stars and other objects that are in the universe.

observatories: Special buildings where astronomers study stars and planets.

Ph.D.: The highest degree a university can award; it stands for Doctor of Philosophy.

physics: A field of science that studies the forces and interactions of everything in the universe.

planetariums: Buildings or rooms in which images of stars and planets are shown on a high, curved ceiling.

power grids: Networks that carry power from suppliers to users.

simulate: Model a situation using a computer.

solar system: The sun and the planets that move around it.

telescopes: Instruments that you look through to see things far away.

universe: Everything in space, including stars, planets, and galaxies.

INDEX

TO LEARN MORE

Learning more is as easy as 1, 2, 3.

1) Go to www.factsurfer.com

2) Enter "astronomer" into the search box.

3) Click the "Surf" button to see a list of websites.

With factsurfer, finding more information is just a click away.